T0091158

Goodbye Sleep

All the Advice I Wish I Got Before Having a Baby

Sam Kaplan, MA & Jesse Barnes, POP

Illustrated by **Kiana Leilani**

Ulysses Press
P.O. Box 3440
Berkeley, CA 94703
www.ulyssespress.com

ISBN 978-1-61243-716-3
Library of Congress Catalog Number: 2017937987

Printed in the United States by Bang Printing
10 9 8 7 6 5 4 3 2 1

Managing Editor: Claire Chun
Project Editor: Alice Riegert
Proofreader: Shayna Keyles
Artwork: © Kiana Leilani except frame © mhatzapa_eps/shutterstock.com

Distributed by Publishers Group West

IMPORTANT NOTE TO READERS: This book is an independent and unauthorized work of parody. No endorsement or sponsorship by or affiliation with any authors, their respective publishers, or other copyright and trademark holders is claimed or suggested. All references in this book to titles, characters, settings, and any other material subject to copyright or trademark are for the purpose of commentary, criticism, and parody only.

To:

The circle of life
Begins with a glance
You lock eyes from afar
And your heart starts to dance.

Butterflies start to flutter
Your palms start to tingle
Oh my! What a fox!
You're so glad that you're single.

But are you ready to mingle?
An approach could be risky
And what will you do
If things start to get frisky?

Put your worries aside
Let your romance take flight
'Cause nothing's as precious
As love at first sight.

The first piece of advice
We would like to impart
Is to cherish your courtship
The second it starts.

Flirt it up, paint the town
Charm the pants off your crush
This newfound infatuation
Is a riveting rush.

Make each moment magic
Make each second splendid
Make each date the grandest
If you don't, you'll regret it!

'Cause the honeymoon portion
The puppy love phase
Is once in a lifetime
(And eventually fades).

A few months fly by
This has far surpassed “fling”
You’re swooning and crooning
Your heart’s all like, “cha-ching!”

Is this the real deal?
Could this one be the one?
You start dreaming of marriage
And daughters and sons.

But don't hop in the fast lane
Please take your sweet time
Let your love-bubble double
And triple in size!

It may be a cliché
But it's still oh-so true
Every family's foundation
Begins just with two….

Most proper proposals
Were probably planned
So put in preparation
To prevent getting panned.

If you want to pass "fling"
Then you must choose a ring
That will fit on her finger
With impeccable bling.

You don't need a big speech
Speak straight from the heart
And whatever you say
Try your best not to fart.

And if your love's true
If your hearts are in line
Then she'll say "Yes! Yes! Yes!"
Or at least she'll say "fine."

The first rules of the game
When it comes time for nuptials:
Avoid stress and feel blessed
Try your best to be punctual.

Just remember your vows
(Or at least say, “I do”)
And don’t have a cow
If one dress isn’t blue.

And maybe, just maybe
The best man and bridesmaid
Will fall madly in love
(Or at least both get laid).

Yes, romance is spreading
There's no need for fretting
Enjoy every last drop
Of your beautiful wedding.

The birds and the bees
Are abuzz and atweet
As you lovebirds retreat
To your honeymoon suite.

It's your very first night
As husband and wife
So whatever you do,
Why not do it twice?

On this special occasion
Your hearts are a'blazin'
Your hormones are ragin':
Commence consummation!

But be wary, my friends
This is well worth stating:
Little babies are born
Nine months after mating....

Just like that, you are preggers!
You're carrying child!
But don't be surprised
If your body goes wild.

Hopefully you're lucky
With no morning sickness
And never get nauseous
Or ill with persistence.

Many soon-to-be-mothers
Begin ranting and raving
And having the oddest
Of feelings and cravings.

“Bring me citrus!” they shout,
“Pickles! Ice cream! More chocolate!”
And our advice to you, Hubbie:
Just try not to drop it.

Things will get real
When you start third-trimesting
For this is the time
When most couples start nesting.

Investing in
Blankies and bottles and binkies
And researching "baby"
And "fresh baby stinkies."

But don't take them for granted
These last baby-free days—
Go on impromptu outings
And romantic getaways.

And last but not leastly
Sleep when you're sleepy
'Cause when the child comes
Your sleep will be measly.

You may start to freak out
As your due date grows closer.
Will your baby get sick?
Or burnt by the roaster?

Your house starts to glow
With a menacing sheen.
You grow fearful of steps
And of every machine.

Electrical sockets
Are incredibly scary,
You start noticing germs.
Are all pets this darn hairy?

But don't hurry or worry
If you don't babyproof:
For the first several months
Babies don't really move.

First comes the water
And next the contractions.
It's time to get focused
No time for distractions!
You can hire a doula
To help you stay calm
While the capable doctor
Performs with aplomb.

And one universal
During every delivery
Is things will get messy
And nitty and gritty.

It's for this very reason
Most men say for certain
To never, oh never,
Go south of the curtain.

Your baby is here!!!
And looks just like a model!!!
Or are you just wearing
Your new parent goggles?

See, all babies are born
With contortions and bumps
And wrinkles on wrinkles
And flaps on their rumps.

They've got hairs on their arms
But none on their heads
And they're blue when their born
(That don't mean that they're dead).

But yours is so beautiful,
Precious, and wise
You can tell that they're perfect
Just look in their eyes.

When you take baby home
It'll take some adjusting
So here's a few tips
To avoid self-combusting.

Well, first we suggest
That you pre-prep your pets
By bringing them sniffs
Of your new infant's scent.

Next, don't be alarmed
When your pooping machine
Makes watery poops that are
Yellow or green.
Most of all, please don't fret
If you struggle adapting
You've got a new boss
Who keeps crying and crapping.

Now it's time to address
The small issue of sleep.
You'll soon find no use
In the counting of sheep.

Your house is now filled
At all hours of night
With the gut-wrenching waaaahs
That might give you a fright.

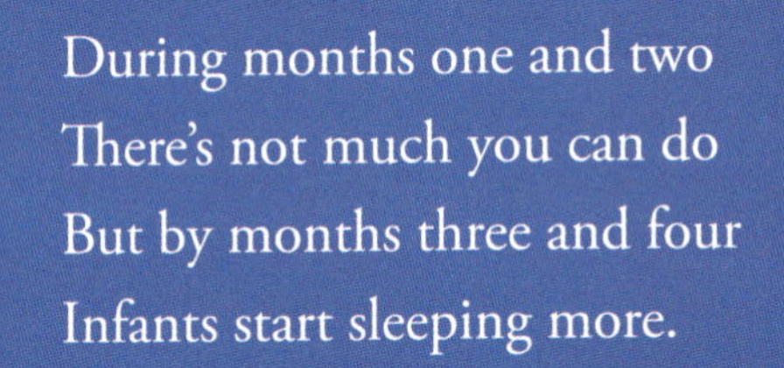

During months one and two
There's not much you can do
But by months three and four
Infants start sleeping more.

So please cherish each nap
And remember this tidbit:
You're just losing your sleep
'Cause you're loving your infant.

What is the baby,
This miniature creature?
It looks like a human
With all the right features.

But its vision is blurry
Its hearing atrocious;
It just sleeps and poops
Even if it's precocious.

But its muscles are growing
It's learning to babble;
Your baby's a genius
Is it time yet for Scrabble?

Your job early on
Is to bond, love, and snuggle.
You can't spoil a baby—
Love's the magic of muggles.

We don't mean to get nerdy
And talk about science
But babies change brainses
And the hormones inside us.

Yes, both Mom and Dad
May approach overdosing
On the lovey-dove hormone
We call oxytocin.

But the female brain
Is pre-wired to grow
In the amygdala
Where those love hormones go.

So try not to get jealous
If you can't break the grip
Between mommy and child—
They're attached at the hip.

Hey Pops! Step it up!
Your role is emerging:
Dad can be super helpful
With changing and burping.

Spend time with your kid
And give Mommy a rest
You can help with the feeding
Even though you lack breasts.

And it may seem excessive
But most top-notch fathers
Take Baby on strenuous
Two-hour saunters.

We promise your efforts
Are worth double scores:
Cause you're bonding with Baby
While you let Mommy snore.

When your baby's just eaten
And then starts to squirm—
Squirm, squirm, and squirm
Like a human-shaped worm.

It's a pretty good sign
Of a small bit of trouble
'Cause your baby's got
Gastrointestinal bubbles.

Whether over your shoulder
Or set in your lap
Your baby needs burping:
A few gentle back-pats.

Soon baby will burp
And might even barf!
That's why we recommend
Wearing a blankie or scarf....

An inevitable aspect
Of parenting duties
Is cleaning up diapers
Filled with gross pees and poopies.

The statistics are staggering
Year one is absurd.
You'll change 3,000 diapers
And see 1,000 turds.

Our only advice
Is get over yourself
Prepare to get dirty
It's for your baby's health.

And men, don't pretend
Like this job can't be split.
'Cause your "manly" excuses
Are old-fashioned bull…just, come on, dude, don't be a jerk, okay?

We'd like to bring up
A small sensitive issue
So before you read on
Find a napkin or tissue.

We've heard tales of tormented
Husbands and wives,
Who grow sad when they notice
The lack of a love life.

"Is it normal?" you wonder.
We promise it is—
It's hard to feel sexy
While raising a kid.

'Cause you spend all your time
Washing bottles and crap
And when baby's asleep
You pray for your own nap.

The very precarious
Planet outside
Becomes very nefarious
Once Baby arrives.

There are critters and spitters
And darkness and dangers
And an overabundance
Of interested strangers.

Your baby will look at
The sites that they see
With a bounty of wonder
And infectious glee.

So trust us on this one:
Go on, get outside
'Cause while watching the world
Your darling will thrive.

Some parents get rattled
By grandmas and grandpas;
They can be overwhelming
And get stuck in your craw.

Some grandmothers smother
Some grandfathers bother
And tell you what to do
With your own son or daughter.

But they also provide
A small speck of relief
'Cause they've done this before
They've got ancient techniques.

So please try to be patient,
Take a deep breath.
Remember that grandparents
Just want what is best.

Don't make the mistake of
Neglecting your buds
'Cause your buds can become
A babysitter's club.

They might play a bit rough
With your delicate sweetie
And a few in your crew
Might get miffed or quite needy.

That's why some first-time parents
Get sucked into nesting
And forget that their friendships
Can be parenting blessings.

So don't stay home alone
When invited to chillage
And remember that saying:
It takes a whole village.

Your baby begins
On a liquefied diet
Of breast milk or formula
Nothing else—don't you try it.

But around four months in
They'll sit up by themself
Now it's time to start feeding them
Spoonfuls of health.

The transition to solids
Is a messy affair
Your house will grow squalid
With food everywhere.

Get used to the gloop
You better not gripe
Just be equipped with a ton
Of nappies and wipes.

With an infant in tow
Everything becomes tricky
The simplest things
Switch from simple to sticky.

Like on trips—nearby flyers
Will gawk and they'll scowl
And they'll moan on the inside
When your babe starts to howl.

They'll be an extra disturbance
During stretches of turbulence
And despite all your nurturance
You'll incite some perturbances.

So bring Baby's favorite toys
And a bounty of books
And snackpacks and bottles
And learn to avoid looks.

One key is the love
Between Mommy and Pappy
'Cause a baby needs parents
Both loving and happy.

We know that you're feeling
Like your brain's full of mush
Disheveled, disgusting
In desperate need of a brush.

And is this sitter equipped
To provide supervision?
And wouldn't you rather
Just watch television?!

Enough with excuses
Get your love life unstuck
Go on your second first date
Then go home and…pay the sitter
and then hopefully don't wake the baby up
and then pass out because you're so exhausted.

Your baby's first sniffles—
What a worrisome sound!
When baby starts wailing
Your heart starts to pound.

They grow clingy and snuggly
And won't let you go
They're feverish and snotty
Here's what you should know:

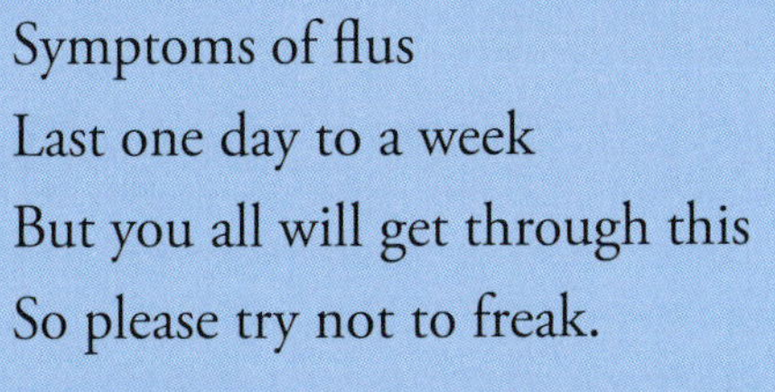

Symptoms of flus
Last one day to a week
But you all will get through this
So please try not to freak.

Call your doc if you're worried
She'll calm you right down
And remember that love
Is the best cure in town.

Your baby is growing
Becoming a person
They're starting to learn
So it's time to stop cursing.

The first several months
Bring a flurry of firsts
From first smiles and giggles
To the first bite of bratwurst.

Soon you'll hear vowels
Emerge from the runt
And a bevy of babbles
And gurgles and grunts.

But nothing's as special
As Baby's first word
Like da-da or ma-ma
Or something absurd.

There's just one last first
That we must bring up
When your baby starts walking
It's lovely and tough.

Your baby's first steps
Are a joyous affair
But along with those steps
Come movements, beware!

Yes, it seems there are jetpacks
Propelling Baby's waddle—
With a mobile bambino
There's no time to dawdle.

Be watchful and wary
And ready to spring
'Cause a baby in motion
Is a precarious thing.

A wondrous day
That's both bitter and sweet
Is the first day of daycare
What a bittersweet treat.

It's not without trials
This time of transition;
Your baby will cry
And forget how to listen.

And look at those toddlers
What perilous monsters!
And those preschool teachers
Look like afternoon sleepers.

But it also means freedom
And a home without small fry
So help them adjust
And then kiss them goodbye.

And wow! Just like that!
You're all done with year one!
You laughed, loved, and cried
And had boatloads of fun.

You sacrificed sanity
But don't get contrite
'Cause now Baby's a toddler
And sleeps through the night!

So hi hubbie, hi wife,
Hi baby-free fiesta!
Hello to snoozeville,
And noontime siesta!

One last piece of advice
We would like to repeat:
Don't you get too romantic
Or again…goodbye sleep!

About the Authors

Sam Kaplan, coauthor of *Goodnight Dorm Room*, is a writer and therapist living in Oakland, California. He enjoys writing about college, poop, and ninjas. As a therapist, he loves working with kids, infants, and families. He has special training in infant mental health. He is currently raising his inner child, who is probably about 3 or 4.

Jesse Barnes lives in Philadelphia with his wife Melanie and their two wonderful children. Three-year-old Owen has a heart of gold and the energy of a caffeinated Tasmanian devil. Eliza is a one-year-old sweetheart who really enjoys getting mush on everything, especially daddy's nicest work clothes. While this is Jesse's first book, he has written at least several mediocre rap songs.

Don't let the names fool you; Sam and Jesse are full-fledged 100% biological brothers.

About the Illustrator

Kiana Leilani draws and journals daily in between making kale chips, shaving yaks, and tending to the cactus plants living underneath her little studio on stilts. She studied painting and illustration at Brigham Young University–Idaho. Kiana now works as a freelance illustrator in Santa Rosa, California, where she lives with her two cats, Kiko and Frog. She is fueled by the growth of getting better at new things and is currently teaching herself yoga, meditation, and how to animate.